Ernest Shackleton

EXPLORING THE SOUTH POLE

Karen Davila

Boston, Massachusetts
Chandler, Arizona
Glenview, Illinois
Upper Saddle River, New Jersey

Illustrations
Opener, 1, 3, 4, 5, 6 London Ladd.

Photographs
Every effort has been made to secure permission and provide appropriate credit for photographic material.
The publisher deeply regrets any omission and pledges to correct errors called to its attention in subsequent editions.

Unless otherwise acknowledged, all photographs are the property of Pearson Education, Inc.

Photo locators denoted as follows: Top (T), Center (C), Bottom (B), Left (L), Right (R), Background (Bkgd)

All Photos: National Library of Australia.

ISBN-13: 978-0-328-67574-6
ISBN-10: 0-328-67574-1

9 10 11 V0FL 16 15 14

A Young Explorer

Ernest Shackleton always loved adventures. His father wanted him to become a doctor, but Shackleton wanted to go to sea. He became a sailor at age 16. He wanted to see the world. He wanted to **explore**.

He joined a trip to the **continent** of Antarctica. It was a cold and hard place to explore. Then he got sick and had to return home to Great Britain. When he got well, he decided to go back to Antarctica.

Trip Leader

Shackleton planned and led his own **expedition** to Antarctica. He came close to the **South Pole**. Later, in Great Britain, he was honored for his bravery as a leader and explorer.

Shackleton planned one more trip to Antarctica. He hoped to get to the South Pole. He also wanted to cross the continent. That was almost two thousand miles! He hoped to study new parts of the continent.

The Hardest Time

The expedition did not go well. Shackleton's ship, the *Endurance*, got stuck in packed ice. The group was trapped for many cold months.

They had to wait for spring and melting ice. Then something worse happened. The *Endurance* sank!

Now, Shackleton had to get his **crew** home. The way to safety was hard and dangerous. But Shackleton never gave up. He got the entire crew home safely. Shackleton was a great leader and brave explorer.

Glossary

continent a very large piece of land

crew the people who work on a ship or expedition

expedition a long trip with a special goal

explore to look for new places

South Pole the farthest point south on Earth